Dr Jenner and the Cow Pox

written by Herbie Brennan

illustrated by Andrew Quelch and James Sneddon

Contents

Young Edward Jenner	2
The deadly disease	4
Variolation	5
Jenner's studies	7
The cow pox cure	8
Doctor Jenner	10
The experiment	12
What doctors thought	14
The method spreads	16
Jenner's last years	18
Vaccination today	20
Timeline	22
Glossary	23
Index	24

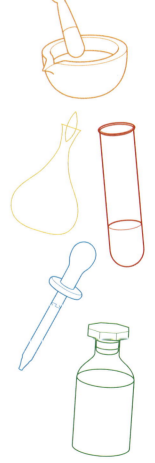

Young Edward Jenner

Edward Jenner was born on 17 May 1749 in Berkeley, Gloucestershire, England. He was the youngest son of the vicar of Berkeley.

Berkeley was a pleasant place to live and Edward quickly grew to love nature and the countryside. He was interested in these things all his life.

The house where Edward Jenner was born.

When Edward was five, both his parents died. After that he was brought up by an older brother, who was a vicar like his father. When Edward was seven, he nearly died too.

The deadly disease

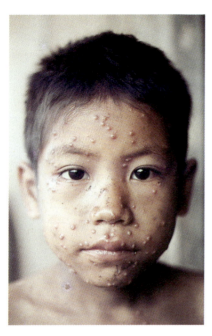

A victim of smallpox

In the eighteenth century everyone in England was afraid of a disease called **smallpox**. People who caught it became very ill with a high fever. After two days their skin would be covered with sores full of pus.

Most people who caught the disease died. Those people who didn't die were often left with ugly **pock marks** on their skin.

Variolation

There was no known cure for smallpox at that time. But there was a treatment to try to stop people catching the disease. A doctor would:
- make a scratch on the patient's arm with a needle
- put liquid from a smallpox scar into the scratch.

In this way, the patient would catch a mild form of smallpox, then get better and never catch the disease in the future.

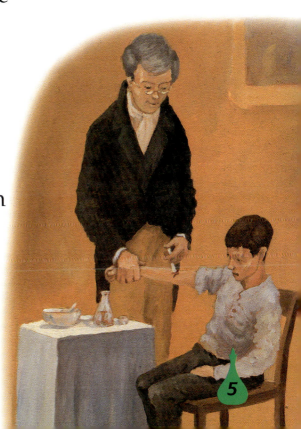

This treatment was called "**variolation**," because the medical name for smallpox is "variola," but it had one big problem. Sometimes the patients did not catch a mild form of smallpox at all. Sometimes the patients died.

This is what very nearly happened to Edward Jenner when he was seven years old. After the variolation treatment he was very ill indeed. Luckily, he did get better, but he never forgot how close he came to death.

Jenner's studies

When he was about thirteen, Edward became an **apprentice** to a local doctor. Over the following eight years, he learned about surgery and medicine. He continued his nature studies and spent as much time as possible in the countryside.

The cow pox cure

One day, when Edward was in the countryside, a milkmaid told him about **cow pox**.

Cow pox sores on a milkmaid's hand

Cow pox was a disease that milkmaids sometimes caught from the cows they milked. It was a mild illness that soon went away.

But many milkmaids believed that if they had caught cow pox, they could never catch smallpox.

Doctor Jenner

In 1770, Edward went to London to work in St George's Hospital where he was trained by the most famous surgeon in the country.

Edward stayed in London for two years before going home to work in Berkeley.

He was a very good doctor and many people came to see him. Some of them had smallpox and there was very little he could do to help them.

Then he remembered what the milkmaid had told him years before when he was training.

In London, Dr Jenner had learned that real scientists don't just think about the problems they face. They do experiments to try and find out the truth.

The experiment

To find out if what the milkmaid had told him was really true, Dr Jenner decided to try an experiment.

A reconstruction of Dr Jenner's experiment

On 14 May 1796, he took some material from an old cow pox scar on the hand of a milkmaid. He put it into the arm of an eight-year-old boy called James Phipps.

A sore came up on the boy's arm, but it healed in two weeks. He hardly became ill at all.

Then Dr Jenner put material from a smallpox scar into James' arm.

He hoped that, if James had caught cow pox, he would not catch smallpox. If he was wrong, then the boy might become seriously ill and could die.

But young James did not get the disease. In fact, Dr Jenner had found a way to stop people catching smallpox. He had discovered **vaccination**.

What doctors thought

Dr Jenner wrote a **medical paper** about his experiment, but other doctors did not believe what he said he had done.

But Dr Jenner knew he was right. He wrote a book about his discovery and went to London to find volunteers for his new treatment.

Although there were no volunteers in London, some doctors there decided to try to repeat his experiment. They found it worked!

When Dr Jenner went back to Berkeley, his friends built him a hut in his garden where he could vaccinate poor people in the area free of charge.

People called the hut "The Temple of Vaccina."

The Temple of Vaccina as it looks today.

The method spreads

There were many difficulties at first, but more and more doctors learned Dr Jenner's method and tried it for themselves. They saw that it worked and spread the word to other doctors.

Dr Jenner spent the rest of his life travelling to different countries telling doctors about the cow pox vaccine and how it could be used to stop people from getting smallpox.

In fact, he spent so much time doing this that he had little time left to earn money. He was soon very short of money. The British Parliament had to come to his rescue twice by giving him a **grant**.

Jenner's last years

Dr Jenner's last years were troubled. Despite the grants from Parliament, his money worries continued. His wife, Catherine, whom he had married in 1788, caught a lung disease and died in 1815.

Without her support, Dr Jenner decided to retire from public life. When he died in 1823, many doctors still did not believe in his ideas about vaccination.

Vaccination today

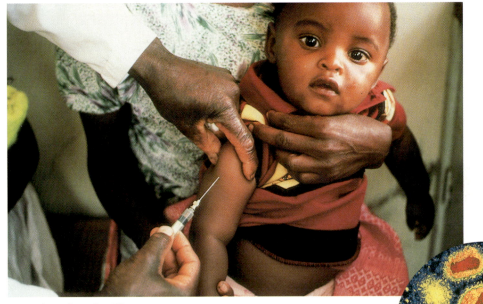

Vaccination in Kenya

In spite of all the difficulties and hardships, Dr Jenner's ideas were proved right at last. As the years went by, it became clear to doctors around the world that vaccination really did work.

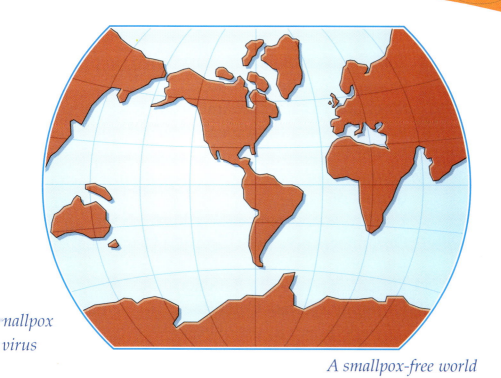

A smallpox-free world

In 1980, the **World Health Organisation** announced that smallpox had been completely wiped out in every country, using the vaccination treatment discovered by Dr Jenner.

Timeline

1000 BC	Earliest cases of smallpox recorded (in China)
710 AD	Smallpox reaches Europe
1520	Smallpox reaches the Americas
1749	Edward Jenner born on 17 May
1754	Edward's parents die
1756	Edward nearly dies from variolation treatment
1762	Edward is apprenticed to a local doctor
1770	Dr Jenner works in St George's Hospital, London
1772	Dr Jenner returns to Berkeley
1788	Dr Jenner marries Catherine
1796	An experiment in vaccination is carried out on James Phipps
1802	Dr Jenner receives his first grant from Parliament
1806	Parliament makes a second grant, twice the size of the first
1815	Dr Jenner's wife dies
1823	Dr Jenner dies
1953	Smallpox vaccination becomes compulsory in Britain
1980	World Health Organisation announces that smallpox has been wiped out

Glossary

apprentice someone who is learning a craft

cow pox a mild disease often caught by milkmaids from the udders of cows

grant gift of a sum of money

medical paper an essay written to tell other medical people about new ideas

pock marks ugly scars left when smallpox sores dry up

smallpox a deadly disease

vaccination giving someone a mild form of a disease to stop them getting a serious form

variolation an early, dangerous type of smallpox vaccination

World Health Organisation a department of the United Nations set up to fight disease

Index

Americas 22
apprentice 7
Berkeley 2, 10, 15, 22
China 22
countryside 2, 7, 8
cow pox 8–9, 12, 13, 16
Europe 22
experiment 11, 12–13, 14, 22
Gloucestershire 2
grant 17, 18
London 10, 11, 14, 22
milkmaid 8–9, 11, 12

Parliament 17, 18, 22
Phipps, James 12–13, 22
pock marks 4
smallpox 4, 5, 6, 9, 11, 13, 16, 21, 22
St George's Hospital 10, 22
surgeon 10
Temple of Vaccina 15
vaccination 13, 15, 16, 19, 20–21, 22
variolation 5, 6, 22
World Health Organisation 21, 22